Just Breathe...

Reflections, Inspirations, and Guidance for Living All the Days of Your Life

Jennifer Todd

*Just Breathe…Reflections, Inspirations, and Guidance
for Living All the Days of Your Life
© 2011 by Jennifer Todd*

*All rights reserved. No part of this book may be used or
reproduced in any manner whatsoever, including Internet
usage, without written consent from Ms. Todd and
jEnergy Publications except in the case of brief, credited
quotations embodied in critical articles and reviews.
www.JustBreatheOrlando.com
www.jEnergyJoy.com*

*Cover, book design and photography
by © Tracy L. Cashon*

Author Photograph by www.Infiniteeverything.net

*ISBN: 978-0-615-54274-4
jEnergy Publications, 2006 Town Plaza Court,
Winter Springs, FL 32708
www.jEnergypublications.com*

Dedication

To Brian...for loving all my Parts (even Ducky). This kind of love is what I dreamed about...thank you.

To my wise and beautiful children, Sara, Cole and Ember...

And to Keri for all the barking, clucking, and flapping, and for driving me back from Crazyville more times than I can count.

Contents

Introduction 3

Power Up! 7

Feelings 31

Awareness 59

Wisdom 81

Distractions 111

Relationships 129

Compassion 167

Introduction

Introduction

A few years ago I heard about a phenomenon known as social media marketing and started a little Facebook page called Just Breathe... as a space to share blurbs of inspiration and promote my practice. My first 5 fans were family and friends and my posts were either quotes from other people or tentative attempts at inspiring others in 240 characters or less. As with most things, the beginning was a bit shaky. However, as I continued to grow, so did the page and it eventually morphed into a (surprisingly) important part of my personal journey. When I felt sad, I talked about it. When I felt like Wonder Woman, I talked about it. Through the feedback I began to realize that (gasp!) other people felt the same things I was feeling, and that we all felt a sense of relief in knowing that we were not alone.

The phrase "Just Breathe..." means so many things to me, but mostly it's a gentle reminder to pause and come back to myself. My hope is that you will read this book with that idea in mind for you. Read it straight through, flip to a specific section or just let the pages fall open and see what the Universe thinks you need to read today. However you choose to use it, I hope it provides as much inspiration and comfort for you as it has for me.

Remember to breathe, my friends...
Jennifer

Power Up!

You are so amazing! You are smart and kind and powerful beyond your imagination. You are beautiful and passionate and miraculous. Yes, YOU...I'm talking to YOU. Just for this moment, close your eyes and see if you can feel how fabulous you are. Not for WHAT you do, but for WHO you are, exactly AS you are. Now remember...it doesn't matter what happens out there, you know the truth...you ROCK!! ♥

We look at everything through our own lens...some days our lens is clouded over with anger or fear, other days it's rose colored with love. Either way, everything that happens 'out there' is irrelevant... it's which lens we are looking through that drives our reactions and therefore, our reality. For today, remember, you have the power to change your reality at any time...just pick up a new pair of glasses!

There is a big difference between "I have to" and "I choose to". We always have choices. Always. We just don't always like what we choose so it's easier to blame our partners, our kids, our boss, or the universe. But when we do that, we hand over our power and then wonder why we feel so resentful. For today, watch your words... shift your perspective and take back your power. I CHOOSE...

While we are powerless to control what happens "out there", you, and you alone, have control over how you will respond. You have the power to choose to be present in your life...to create a positive, safe environment...to surround yourself with beauty and light. Every day, you choose the life you want. So, for today...plant your feet firmly on the ground, take a deep breath and choose wisely, my friends.
Choose love. ♥

For today, stand a little straighter, smile a little brighter, be a little bolder...because YOU are a powerhouse! You are infinite, amazing, powerful and gorgeous. You are a child of the Universe and for that alone, you deserve to be a little sassy today. So, head up...shoulders back...big breath... go get 'em!!

For today, take a moment and think about what you want your life to look like. Be specific. Just for right now put fear and doubt aside and remind yourself that your possibilities are endless...boundless...you can be, do, and have whatever you want. There is no one more powerful in your life than you. Breathe in that Truth and go make yourself a fabulous day!

When we use words like "I can't", we are again making ourselves the victim..."I can't" tells us we are trapped. There is a huge difference between "I can't" and "I don't want to". For today, when you hear yourself saying that you "can't", remember that YOU are in charge. If you really don't want to, then don't...but know that it's your choice and that you do have options. Power up, baby!

Remember the days when we blamed everyone else for our unhappiness, for our crazy, for our choices? Ah...the good old days...but were they really? Even though it's hard, there's nothing more empowering than realizing YOU hold the key to your happiness, your sanity, your choices. When we blame others for our lack, we make ourselves the victims. For today, put on your superhero cape and practice your power moves. Shazam!

*"Man stands in his own shadow
and wonders why it's dark."
~Zen Proverb.
The only thing holding you back is
you...Ask yourself how often you
say "yeah, but" or "if only" or
"I can't". It's not easy, but anything
is possible. For today, dare to be
remarkable...dare to be YOU!!*

I don't think you realize how powerful you really are. You might look at other people and see their passion, intelligence and potential and think, "wow" but then look in the mirror and say, "yuck." At the risk of repeating myself...you are amazing!! And best of all, you have everything you need, right now. For today, light your own fire... look in the mirror and be wow-ed by YOU. Fire it up, baby!

*Watching our words today...
another powerful phrase is I AM.
We use these two tiny words
without thought, but they have
power far beyond their size. How
do you define yourself?
i am FAT...
i am STUPID...
i am TRAPPED?
For today, let's practice the power
of positive-pick one and let it be
your mantra:
i am POWERFUL.
i am BEAUTIFUL.
i am FABULOUS.
i am PASSIONATE.
i am LUCKY.
i am FREE.
I AM LOVE.* ♥

What would your life be like if you believed you could do anything? Just for today, put your "yeah, buts" and "if only's" aside and ask yourself who you really want to be. You are infinitely more powerful than you imagine and you have everything you need within you. The trick is having the courage to step out of your own way. Big breath...now go get 'em!

You deserve to be happy, to live in abundance, freedom, love and peace. The catch is that no one can give you any of these things... you have to choose them for yourself and then practice living there. Life happens all around us...circumstances can be good or bad...but how we live our life is our choice. Every second that ticks by is an opportunity for love, happiness, balance. For today, what will you choose?

Fairy tales teach us that if we're "good" enough, then our knight in shining armor will come rescue us from our loneliness, from our sorrow. Some people wait their entire lives for that one special person to "save" them. The truth is that no one can save you...but you. How empowering to realize that YOU hold the key to your happiness...the cure to your loneliness. Your knight in shining armor is...YOU...saddle up!

Taking responsibility for ourselves means no more blaming others for our agitation, for our situations, for our lack. I remember the days when I blamed my job for my stress, my ex for my bad moods and the economy for my finances. The problem with all that blaming is that nothing ever changed for me...and I was the Victim. Today I know that I alone am responsible for my life. Period. That, my friends, is Power.

Sometimes life feels so overwhelming and I find myself with a "when it rains, it pours" mentality. Then a wise woman showed me the victim pattern in that attitude. Yes, life happens, but my external life is a mirror of what's happening on the inside. It's much more empowering to remember that I choose what I bring in to my life...then I can shift my thought patterns and attitude instead of sitting in the pouring rain.

We are a society of blamers-we run ourselves into the ground at work and blame the boss; we bend over backwards until we can bend no more in our relationships and then blame our partners. We feel as if we have "no choice." Good news: everything is a choice. Not just some things...Every Thing. Just for today, try that radical concept on for size. YOU get to choose everything for you. Isn't it exciting? Empowering?

Today I own that my choices have led me here. Every twist, every turn, every up, every down... my choices. Things do not happen TO me...the circumstances of my life are direct consequences of MY choices. When I feel happy and balanced, it's a clue that my choices have been in a direction that serves my higher good. When I feel resentful, it's a clue that perhaps I may need to choose a different direction. What will you choose today?

"It takes courage to grow up and become who you really are."
~e.e. cummings.
I love this quote...it takes courage to stop blaming other people or circumstances or life for your situation. It takes courage to take responsibility for yourself...your actions, your words, your choices. But if you can find that courage, the rewards are huge. Victims have no power...take yours back.

Smile...you are fabulous! Laugh... you are miraculous! Hold your head up high...you are so powerful. For today, decide that you are amazing and LIVE like it. ♥ *You are infinitely powerful...so wise, so intuitive...your gut instinct, your wise inner voice, your higher self that just KNOWS. No matter how many times you've ignored her... she is always with you...sometimes with a whisper, sometimes with a two by four to the head. The answers you need are already there...just not "out there"... you've got it all inside. Shhhh...listen...*

YOU are a miracle. Yes, you! Just think about everything that had to happen...all the stars that had to align...for you to be exactly who you are, doing what you are doing, at this very moment. For today, take a moment to really breathe that in...the fact that you matter...that you are amazing, just as you are and just because you are.

Are you excited about your life? I know, I know...you're saying, "what's to be excited about? I get up, blah, blah...I go to work, blah, blah...I cook dinner, blah." Try a new perspective...think of all the amazing opportunities you have. You got up...FABULOUS!! You got dressed...AWESOME!! For today, even though it might feel silly, show some enthusiasm about the little things...get excited about your life!

Feelings

I'm great at diagnosing other people...one of my gifts is being able to cut straight to the chase and get to the point of the issue. Professionally, this is fabulous...personally, not so much. I use diagnosing as a way to focus on everyone but myself. As I become aware of it, I can gently remind myself that I'm most likely trying to "diagnose" away MY feelings and pause for a breath to see where I am.
Key word = gently.

Had a disagreement with a bathing suit recently and unfortunately, the bathing suit won. It never ceases to amaze me how mean I can be to myself. Ultimately, I was able to find my adult and reel in the negative self-talk but it was still painful. Our thoughts and words are so powerful and they have a real impact on our precious little souls...for today, see if you can turn your negative words into kind ones.

How many times have you not given yourself permission to cry because you were afraid that once you start, you'll never be able to stop? These "heavy" emotions feel so big sometimes and they scare us. For today, remember that, just like everything else, this too shall pass and the sun will come out tomorrow. ♥

Let's try an experiment today...every time you hear yourself say the word "should" (or "shouldn't"), stop for a moment and ask yourself "WHY?". Whose voice is that? Is it fear? Insecurity? Shame? Instead of berating yourself for how you should and shouldn't feel, see if you can allow yourself to just be. Our judgment of ourselves is half the pain...and it's so not necessary!

We're quick to tell ourselves what we can't do...what we don't like...what we can't have. Our words are one of our most powerful tools (or weapons!)...so listen to yourself...and pick up those pom poms. For today, be your own biggest cheerleader and focus on what you CAN do, what you DO like and what you already have. And if you hear that voice telling you NO...cheer louder...because you've got SPIRIT, baby, yes you DO!

As you go throughout your day today...remember...your words are beyond powerful. Instead of "I can't", try "of course I can". Instead of "ugh, I'm miserable" try "I am so comfortable in my body". YOU get to choose how you feel, think and interact with the rest of the world. It all starts with you...so, take a deep breath and go get 'em!

My recovering control freak is flying her flag today! It's a good reminder that, although I don't let her drive my bus anymore, she's always there, waiting to offer her "assistance"...especially when I get scared. And today, I am scared, so my instinct is to control, go, do, fix! But I know none of that serves my greater good, so instead I choose to breathe...and let go...and trust that I'll be ok, no matter what.

"You taught me to be nice, so nice that now I am so full of niceness, I have no sense of right and wrong, no outrage, no passion."
~Garrison Keillor.

How many times do you smile over your true feelings because they're not nice? Part of growing up and becoming who we really are is looking at what we were taught and determining whether those lessons still serve us. Life is messy...grab a tissue and find your passion!

We struggle with "negative" emotions-running from them, using whatever we can to push them away. The irony is that the methods we use to avoid them can, in the end, be more destructive than the actual feeling. For today, try "inviting the feeling in for tea"...instead of rejecting it, try embracing the emotion and feeling it. Yes, it may be painful in the moment, but just breathe...and trust that this too, shall pass.

Feelings

Why it is so hard to trust ourselves? We have everything we need right there inside of us, and yet we constantly disregard our inner voice and look for answers in books, websites, gurus, talk shows, family. Just for today, let's all take a moment to breathe in, ask our question and see what we have to say. Maybe we will be surprised!

Had a pretty harsh wake-up call regarding something in my life I've been trying hard to live in denial about. Inner wisdom starts out as a whisper and then eventually gives a good, hard whack to the back of the head. My denial does not mean I'm a horrible person...it means that I wasn't ready to see what I wasn't ready to see. For today, I'll gently lift my head out of the sand and see what I can do differently. ♥

Now that we've decided to FEEL, the next question is always, "what do I DO with the sad? I've been sad for like an hour and I still feel terrible...make it stop!" Then we go right back to all the ways we tried to run from the feeling in the first place. I can't mope around all day...I've got a life! The answer is that this is a process. We don't feel our entire sadness in an hour...let yourself cry until you're ready to stop. It doesn't have to be all or nothing...tomorrow is another day.

I am a BIG believer in the power of our thoughts and words. I believe in the power of intention and positive affirmations. However... all the positive thinking in the universe cannot erase our core beliefs. The power of the positive is amazing, but we still have to heal the "uckies", as well. For today, I tell myself that I'm beautiful and then work on healing the part of me who believes that I'm not. ♥

Woke up today feeling small and overwhelmed, hearing the words, "I don't know what to do". I've learned those words are code for "I want to make the bad feelings STOP" and that if I'm able to get quiet and breathe, I usually DO know what to do. Just for today I'm sad and a little scared and even though I don't like those feelings, I know this too shall pass and that I can be gentle with myself until the sun comes out again.

I have a choice. I can choose to continue old patterns or I can choose to take tentative, unsure steps toward a new opportunity. The hard part is that I KNOW the old way...it might be painful, but it's comfy and familiar. The new path is unknown...I have no idea what's coming. So for today I will honor the part of me that's scared and then take a deep breath and ask the Universe to help guide me as I start up the new road.

I'm working on re-defining what love means to me. I think my definition of love has been a little dysfunctional at times and has led to some pretty unfulfilling relationships. As I grow and learn, I know it's time to let go of old parameters. Out with the old, in with the new! Can you think of anything in your life that needs re-defining?

"No matter where you go, there you are."~Confucius.
Some days I imagine running away to an island and living in a cave just to get away from my life...it's a nice fantasy, but the truth is that my LIFE is not the issue...it's ME. I am the common denominator in all of my relationships and dramas (big and small) and when I lose myself in those things I lose balance and peace. For today, breathe...and find yourself.

Why do we say yes when we mean no? We are the "nice" one, the one who handles stuff, we smile pretty and give people what they want. Everybody loves us! Right? The problem here is that we cannot continuously put ourselves last without eventually feeling angry and resentful. Then we get snarky, blow up and head to crazy-ville. Whoops! For today, imagine saying no when you want to and wonder how your life would be different.

If you know me personally, you know I love to talk! One of my most difficult lessons has been to slow down and get quiet. I use talking as a delightful distraction... if I'm scared, I'll just talk faster and if I'm sad, I'll just smile and ramble on and no one will know! I talked myself right out of every heavy emotion I had and I suffered for it. Surprise...when I stopped talking, I started feeling. So, just for today...shhh.

There is a Zen story about a man who is so terrified of his shadow that he spends his entire life frantically trying to run from it. He wastes his life trying to get away from this part of himself, when all he really needed to do was sit down under a tree. For today, ask yourself what part you are running from and try to remember that EVERY part of you deserves love and compassion. Even (especially) the shadows.

How many times throughout your day do you apologize for yourself? We say "I'm sorry" for our feelings, for asking questions, for changing our minds, for our decisions, for our very existence. Our words (inside and out) are so powerful, yet we are locked into these scripts without even being aware of it. For today, remember that you do not need to apologize for who you are, what you feel or what you need. Own it!

Imagine your inner self as a room that started out with clean, white walls. Then people wrote upon those walls things they believed to be true about us. Eventually, we took up the paintbrush and added our own beliefs...not all of them kind. As adults, it's our job to decide which beliefs serve our greater good and which we are ready to let go. For today, take a moment to read your walls and then grab a new paintbrush!

Speaking of judging...there's no one who can judge me harsher than me. When we feel like everyone is judging what we do or say...the loudest voice (and usually the ONLY voice) is coming from within. Ask yourself whose voice that really is...and then ask it to take a break. For today, see if you can replace the negative with a positive at least once. Try "I love my curves" instead of "I'm a fat cow". Be nice...to YOU!

We have a tape playing constantly in the background. What is yours saying? We can't change it until we acknowledge it, but it seems that once we listen in, it's all we can hear so we quickly ignore it again. It has actually been there all along, the volume has just been turned down. It's not easy to face the truth...that we are so unkind to ourselves, but once we face it, we can begin to change it.
Be kind to you.

Listen to yourself...no one knows you like you do. Somewhere along the way we have lost contact with that inner voice that guides us when all else fails. We might still hear it, but we are so quick to disregard it and turn to others for direction. We KNOW what we need, be it a new job or more sleep or a different relationship. Breathe in and listen....breathe out and do it.

The next time you are feeling overwhelmed by an emotion, see if you can rate it on a scale of 1 (totally chill) to 10 (running around with your hair on fire). Remind yourself that any emotion over a 5...fear, resentment, anxiety...is not your grown-up, it's one of your little ones pretending to be a grown-up. The emotion may be valid, but the intensity usually comes from a little kid place. Then, put on your Big Kid pants and just breathe...

Awareness

I ask clients, "What do you want?" and the answer is usually, "To be happy." But what does that mean, really? Happiness feels like this destination we're all fighting to get to, but we really have no idea what it is...and in the meantime, amidst all the struggle, we're missing what's happening right in front of us. What if, instead of fighting for what could or should be, we focused on what IS? Hmm...I feel happy!

The best way to prepare for life is to begin to LIVE. Take a moment as you read this to ask yourself if you are truly LIVING or just going through the motions. If you don't like the answer, then for today make just one new choice...for today do just one thing differently...

We pass through life so quickly...our days and weeks and months pass by like a dream as we speed through each day. Before we know it, another year has gone by and we're saying, "where did it go?" Slow down today...breathe. Pay attention to your body, Pay attention to your life. Savor the day!

I've been finding myself worrying a lot lately...trying to figure out how, what, when, where, who... and thanks to a wonderful friend, I remembered what wasted energy that is. When I worry about the future, I miss what's happening NOW and so just for today, I'm choosing to release the worry (aka my attempts to control things!) back to the Universe and enjoy where I am right now.

Life doesn't always have to be so serious or hard...have FUN today, giggle, smile, laugh, turn the music up and SING. Just for today, decide that things are EASY and glide through your day...like you're on a slip n' slide! Wheeee!!

Sometimes we get so caught up in what we don't have, what we can't do...who we aren't...that we forget how funny life is. It's so easy to get annoyed and stay that way, but just for today...lighten up! So, you're stuck in traffic? Who cares...turn up the music and boogie down. Or better yet, turn the music down and sing your OWN song out loud! ♥

When things in our life get hard...losing a job, a relationship, an illness...it's so easy to get caught up in "crazy" thinking. We spin OUT of control trying TO control our situations, our minds going a million miles an hour...I should have said this, what does it mean, what will I do? Sometimes the best thing to do is stop, let go and breathe... trust that you will be ok today, no matter what.

Awareness

For today, allow yourself to be wherever you are and to feel whatever you feel. So much of our energy is spent trying to talk ourselves into or out of feelings. If you're happy...BE happy. If you're sad...BE sad. In other words...just breathe...♥

I think of the Law of Attraction like a giant Bat Signal...we are constantly sending a vibrational request out into the Universe and its frequency is based on our feelings, desires, beliefs. That's great when I'm peaceful, loving and Zen, but what about when I'm, well...less than Zen? No need to paste a fake smile on our faces...just like us, the Universe is made up of light and dark and tomorrow is another day!

Sometimes we get the biggest results from the smallest changes. The idea is to set yourself up for success. It would be delightful to sit and meditate for 3 hours a day, but seriously...I have a life. So for today, I will appreciate the quiet times I can find throughout my day and use them to the fullest. It doesn't have to be complicated...

"If you understand, things are just as they are; if you do not understand, things are just as they are."
~ Zen Proverb.

For today, see if you can practice just being in the moment...each moment, as it comes. Give your brain a rest from trying to figure it all out and just breathe...

Awareness

In the midst of your busy life... rush here, clean this, pick up here, cook this...remember you. Even if you give yourself just 5 minutes here and there to close your eyes and breathe...to stand for 2 more minutes under the hot shower all by yourself...to sit in the car and finish singing that song that makes you smile...to savor that cup of coffee. In every way, it's the little things that matter. ♥

I'm working hard these days to stay in the present moment...as a recovering control freak I have a tendency to think everything to death and when I do that, I always end up making myself crazy! I'm learning that it's not about the "what if"...it's about the "what now" and that since I only get one shot at this life, this moment, I don't want to miss a thing. For today...enjoy your NOW...you only get one.

Living consciously does not mean being perfect...it means being aware of our imperfections and loving ourselves anyway. It means being present in our bodies so that they can communicate with us, even when it's painful. It means laughing when we're happy, screaming when we're angry and crying when we're sad. It's LIVING our lives awake and making plenty of mistakes along the way...now that's perfection!

I'm learning (again!) to get out of my own way and just let things unfold. Control is an illusion...no matter how much I worry or analyze, things work out just like they're supposed to. And the good news is that what the Universe has in store for me usually exceeds my wildest imagination anyway. So (again!), for today, I will just breathe...stay in the present moment and trust that I'm right where I'm supposed to be.

You have chosen to be in this body, on this earth, at this time. Open your eyes, breathe, connect and engage...whether you're at the grocery store or holding someone you love...don't sleepwalk through your days. Your life, your time here is so precious. Trust me, you do not want to miss this!

For today, make love a conscious choice for yourself. Let the little things roll off your back...it just doesn't matter whether the laundry gets folded and put away...whether someone took your parking place...whether the kids are making a mess. This day, this time is precious. So for today, breathe... slow down and be present in your life. You have so much to be thankful for!

You do not have to hold your breath and watch your life from the sidelines...you do not have to wait until you get a better job or a partner or more money...you can choose to get present in your life and start living, no matter what your situation. Conscious living does not wait until "one day"...it begins right now as you are reading this. For today, remember to breathe and that this is your life, so live it!

Found myself feeling resentful last night...in that place where if one more person asks me to do something I think I'll start screaming and never stop!! Instead of starting an eternal scream, I decided to breathe. Surprise! I haven't been taking very good care of myself...I had slipped back into the martyr role. Sigh. For today, I'm thankful that I'm aware of my choices so that I can make new ones.

We sometimes find ourselves getting stuck in an event...what he said, what she said. We replay the event over and over, we make ourselves crazy trying to "figure" it out. Why? As humans, we like action! Sitting with emotion, with the uncomfortable is hard, so we tell ourselves to suck it up, to make a plan, to make it better! Whoa, Nelly...don't forget to breathe...slow down, and allow yourself to feel.

Wisdom

I love kaleidoscopes...you can be looking through one at a particular scene and then all it takes is a slight turn and the whole picture completely changes. Hmmm... anyone else sensing a metaphor, here? Of course...perspective is everything. When we look at our lives we may see sorrow, missed opportunities, and broken hearts...but, slight turn to the right, please...now we see how all of those "mistakes" led us to wisdom, better opportunities, and new relationships. Ta da!

Out with the old, in with the new doesn't mean that we slam the door on our past and act like it didn't happen. While it is important to let things go, in order to do that we must acknowledge our sadness or anger...allow ourselves to just be there for a bit and then accept that what happened, happened and it's over now. When we ignore our feelings we will repeat the same patterns...feeling allows us to heal and move forward.

We don't gain confidence by being perfect...we grow by falling down and then getting back up. I am human...I will make "mistakes". I will choose bumpy roads and fall down into ditches. But I don't have to stay down there. I know how to climb back up, clean myself off and choose a new path. Just for today, take a big breath and let yourself fall...knowing beyond a shadow of a doubt that you will stand up stronger and wiser.

Courage doesn't mean living with no fear...it means feeling the fear, acknowledging it and continuing to move forward in spite of it. For today, see if you can take some steps toward freedom...step outside of your box, share an intimate moment with someone you love, take a risk, speak up. Let freedom ring!

We get frozen by fear...we're afraid to make a decision, afraid we'll do the wrong thing, afraid to get hurt. Ack...my chest hurts already! Breathe...it's ok. Unless we're performing brain surgery or diffusing a bomb, nothing we do is forever. No matter how far down the path you have traveled, you can always turn around. Sometimes we just have to take a step...and then another. You've totally got this...

When we are unable to use our voice to say no and to set boundaries, our bodies will find a way to do it for us. Anxiety, migraines, fibromyalgia, back pain...the list goes on. We don't WANT to allow ourselves to be pulled in a million directions or to sacrifice ourselves for others. But we do...because saying NO is scary. For today, ask yourself if your body is the one saying no for you and get curious about why. ♥

You deserve to be treated with kindness and compassion...you deserve love and joy and abundance in all things. Oh dear, I can almost hear the "yeah, buts"...it's so hard for us to hear that we deserve good things. We can believe it for others, but will give a million reasons why we "can't". Give yourself this day to expect and allow the good things...they're always there, we just need to open up and receive them!

Wondering...for whom do we live our life? Do we live for our parent's approval? For our partner and children? For our jobs? Stepping outside of others' expectations for us takes immense courage and faith, but ultimately, that's what growing up is all about. We live for ourselves...we follow our own guidance. For today, grab your big kid pants and try not to worry so much about what everyone else is thinking.

At the core of all of us lies the deep seated fear that we are not enough...not good enough, not smart enough, not, not, not. To compensate for what we perceive to be our lack we may overachieve, trying to be everything to everyone to "prove" our worth. For today, ask yourself how this fear shows up in your life, and remember that nothing "out there" can fill that void. Your worth comes from within.

Wisdom

One does not go to the mountain to find their peace...One brings their peace to the mountain.
~ Zen proverb.
You have everything you need to be peaceful and happy. It's not about what's "out there"...you've already got it. For today, remember to turn your gaze inward...that's where all your wisdom lives.

Resolutions...whether you want to lose weight, strengthen your spiritual practice, clean out your closets or find a partner...the idea is to set yourself up for success. That begins with the words you use to set your intention. "I don't want to be alone" is very different than "I want my life to be filled with loving, positive, powerful people." Focus on what you DO want...then bring the positive in!

Wisdom

Today is the first day of the rest of your life...fill it with light, love, laughter, compassion, gentleness and joy. And as always...don't forget to breathe...♥

"When written in Chinese, the word "crisis" is composed of two characters - one represents danger and the other represents opportunity." ~JFK.
How many opportunities have we missed because we were frantically reacting to "danger"? We freeze, forget to breathe and then flail about trying to make it stop. Just for today, slow down, breathe and turn your kaleidoscope one click to the right. It's a whole new perspective!

The last time I was sick, I stayed home, took my herbs, slept, said positive affirmations, and meditated...and, yet I woke up the next morning still not feeling well. In our society of instant gratification, we get annoyed when we don't see instant results. I did everything I was supposed to, so WHY don't I feel better? Healing is a process...whether it's physical or emotional. Our lives are in the journey, not the destination. ♥

"Speak your truth, even if your voice shakes." ~Maggie Kuhn. Being vulnerable is a very scary thing! We're afraid of judgment... or worse, rejection. So we put on a brave face and say we're fine. Or we stay so busy taking care of everyone else that we don't have time to think about ourselves. But we all deserve to have a voice...the question is, are we brave enough to use it?

Wisdom

Our time here is so precious...just for today, take a risk, do something different, or do nothing at all, but no matter what, be present in your life. Don't just phone it in, turn off your auto-pilot and take the wheel. Make eye contact. Listen. Hug. See and be seen. Love. ♥

Some days we take two steps forward and some days we take two steps back...or three or twelve. I'm learning that MY idea of what things should look like is sometimes not the same as the Universe's and that there is peace in knowing that everything is going to work out just like it is supposed to - with or without my input. For today, I'm choosing step out of my own way and go with the flow. In other words...Just Breathe...

Peace begins within. When I come from a place of inner peace, I see peace all around me. The sky is brighter, people are more kind, even traffic moves better. Breathe in the light today, breathe out the dark...what does your world look like when you come from a place of peace?

I have a shoe rule: I won't buy new shoes unless I'm willing to let go of an old pair. I'm not big on rules in general, but this one is helpful in keeping balance and harmony in my closet. The concept is true outside my closet, too. Many times I have to let go of something "old" in my soul to find balance and harmony, to open the way for new things. Letting go of things is sometimes painful but I do love new shoes!

Many times, our bodies will try to set boundaries for us that we are unable to set for ourselves. If you often find yourself sick and tired with headaches, back pain, stomach issues, etc., ask yourself what your body is trying to tell you. Are you unable to say no? Are you choosing to put work, school, friends or family first and forgetting to take care of yourself? Just breathe... and listen to your body.

Focusing on our vocabularies today...we tell ourselves we are "good" or "bad", "right" or "wrong"...what if there WAS no good/bad, right/wrong and just us - living our lives to the best of our abilities? Would you do things differently?

Today we practice peace. Close your eyes and remember a time when you felt that all was right with the world. Perhaps you were sitting on your porch sipping the perfect cup of coffee or holding your child while she slept or laughing with friends. Feel the fullness of your heart, the calmness of your mind, the stillness of your body. Breathe. Whenever you are feeling lost you can practice returning to this place.

Have you ever woken up feeling incredibly blessed and grateful for the love in your life? Wouldn't it be cool if we could feel like that all the time? Just for a moment, close your eyes, take a deep breath in and allow yourself to feel all the love surrounding you. Even when you feel completely alone, all you really need to do is reach into the Energy that surrounds you to feel love. See if you can wrap it around yourself like a warm, fuzzy blanket today and then share it!

How would your life be different if you had a fairy godmother following you around...speaking up for you, protecting you, making sure that every choice served your higher purpose? You would have less anxiety, more confidence...you would feel happy and free, yes? Well, good news, kiddos! You've got it... the only catch is that your fairy godmother is YOU. So for today, wave your magic wand and choose you...alacazam!

The most important thing for you to do right now is simply follow your heart. Do what you love and associate yourself with people you love and respect the most. Oh, yes...and don't forget to breathe.

Take a moment to bring your awareness to your body. Are you in pain? Do you feel tightness or anxiety? Breathe in and imagine a healing light flooding your body, sweeping away pain and anxiety. Breathe out and imagine all of the negative energy flowing out of your body in a cloud of black smoke. Breathe in light, breathe out dark. Pay attention today and breathe when you need to...it's the most powerful tool you have!

*There is a huge difference between taking care of yourself and being "selfish". If you are feeling extra crankypants and resentful and exhausted, ask yourself when you last had a moment for yourself and then go back to the basics: eat well, sleep, breathe...replenish yourself, ask for help. Even if it's just a few moments here and there...
take care of you!*

You know those days where you feel so overwhelmed? Where you don't know which way to turn...don't know what to do...what to feel? Where you get stuck in the "what ifs" and the "I don't knows" so you just do nothing? Hmmm...I'm calling shenanigans! The truth is that when you are able to quiet down the peanut gallery in your head, you DO know. You know exactly what you want to say...exactly how you feel and exactly what you want to change. You just don't WANT to know, so instead you get confused. For today, OWN it. I DO know what to do...I just don't WANT to yet.
Big difference!

Distractions

Woke up this morning with my thoughts going a million miles an hour... what, who, when, how, why? It's so easy to get lost on that hamster wheel and run around frantically trying to "control" everything, however I've learned enough to know that I'm no good to myself or anyone else in that stressed state. So for today, I chose to slow down and breathe for a few minutes and it's amazing how different my day looks! Peace.

Distractions

Speaking of choices...there are no "right" or "wrong" ones. We agonize over our decisions, big and small...wanting to be perfect. Trying to avoid "mistakes", we think things to death. Sometimes the kindest thing we can do for ourselves is stop thinking. You have an innate wisdom that gets drowned out by frantic activity. For today, gently turn down the volume in your head...breathe... and listen to your heart.

Ah, distractions! Some are more socially acceptable than others, but we all use them. Feeling "negative" emotions is difficult and we were not taught how to deal with our anger, fear, sorrow...so we work, shop, care-take, have sex, eat too much, drink or pop a Xanax. It's hard for most of us to stop and just breathe because then we start to feel. The irony is that the only way out...is through.
Keep breathing!

Distractions

Oh, how we worry. The movies that play in our heads are better than anything on the big screen...terrifying, stressful, dramatic to the max! Most times, reality never even comes close to our imaginations. For today, when you find yourself on the hamster wheel, take a moment and breathe...see if you can comfort that part of you who is scared and remember that no matter what, you'll be okay in the end. ♥

I need to be aware of my frantic go, go, go activity...I use it as an escape...it's difficult for me to feel anything when I'm bouncing around like a caffeinated spider monkey. We all have something that we use to get "away" from ourselves. When you find yourself lost in cleaning (work, eating, drinking), see if you can pause for a moment and ask yourself if you're running "away" from something, then put down the scrub brush and breathe.

Distractions

When you find yourself caught up on the hamster wheel of frantic thought, restlessly pacing back and forth in your mind, trying to figure it all out, running down every possibility...shhh....breathe. While all this activity is a lovely distraction and a nice illusion of control, all that wasted energy really gets us nowhere but frustrated. For today, come down out of your head and let your heart be your guide. Breathe...

Stepping outside our comfort zone means relinquishing control, blindly walking into unchartered territory. EEK! I'm off the beaten path right now and all I know to do is keep putting one foot in front of the other. Yes, I'm scared, but there's also a relief in knowing that I don't have all the answers, that's it's not all up to me. Will I get hurt? Maybe...but I'll never know if I don't try.

Distractions

The first time I set an intention to meditate and quiet my mind, I could only tolerate the stillness for about 4 minutes...no kidding. I felt guilty...there was laundry to fold, the kids might need me. I felt annoyed...what's the point of this again? But mostly, I felt afraid...if I stopped moving what would I feel? For today, ask yourself what keeps you in perpetual motion and what might happen if you got quiet. Shhh...

What would it be like to be truly yourself...no excuses, no apologies? What if we could accept ourselves exactly as we are...the good, the bad, the beautiful, the difficult? Imagine the freedom of dropping all the pretenses, of speaking our truth. How much energy we'd have if we stopped trying to hold it all together? For today...just be.

Routines are not a bad thing... they can be comforting, safe. I get up, brush my teeth, have my coffee, etc., etc. But sometimes we get stuck in our comfort zones...we do, say and feel the same things over and over and then we feel frustrated, unfulfilled, bored. For today, try something new: hug someone... just because, eat something different for lunch, change the radio station, be silly. Allow yourself to have FUN!

I found myself spinning through my rolodex of things to worry about this morning...I literally flip through the pages in my mind: work, kids, money, health. I've learned enough about myself to know that worrying is a lovely distraction from some emotion I'm trying to avoid and as soon as I acknowledge it, the spinning slows down. For today, breathe... and ask yourself what your spinning is really all about.

Distractions

No one taught us how to have uncomfortable feelings so we work hard to avoid them...we spin on our hamster wheel trying to find ways to "fix" things (people), we sacrifice ourselves so that others will be happy...thinking that will make US happy. But it doesn't. And we're not. Learning to stop...to just breathe...and sit with our sadness, our anger, our fear is challenging and scary but necessary. For today, I choose to FEEL my feelings instead of running from them. ♥

I have a situation in my personal life that I'm really unhappy about and I've been spinning it around in my head, looking at it from every angle, complaining about it, essentially trying to control things that are impossible to control! A brilliant friend of mine reminded me to stop focusing so much on what I DON'T want and start focusing on what I DO want. Wow. What a difference. Thank you!

Thinking about how we get stuck in cycles...we get frustrated and mad but don't know how to effectively express ourselves in a way that creates change. We give the silent treatment, or smile pretty, or blow up and screech at people, but none of these gets us the change we are looking for and we end up more frustrated. Whew! For today, see if you can get clear about what you want to be different and try a new tactic.

Distractions

Speaking of energy...do you know how much energy it takes to talk yourself out of where you are? So much of our "crazy-making" comes from trying to convince ourselves that we aren't really sad or that we shouldn't be mad...OY VEY. Telling yourself that you aren't angry doesn't make it "go away"...it just makes us feel frustrated and bad about ourselves. For today, try to just let yourself be...♥

Distractions

Decisions can be difficult...we struggle with the weight of making the "right" choice, we analyze everything trying to anticipate each possible outcome. Here's a radical concept...there are no "right" or "wrong" decisions...there is no such thing as a "mistake". Trust yourself enough to know that no matter what you decide, you are right where you are supposed to be and that it's all going to be okay. ♥

Relationships

The more I do this work, the more I realize that we are all fundamentally the same. We may have taken different routes to get here, but we are all driven by a deep fear that we are not enough...that somehow, we are less than. For today, make an effort to SEE your fellow human beings as just that...human. See if you can set aside judgment of yourself and others today and come from a place of compassion. Ready, set...♥!

How do we "protect" ourselves from negative energy? From someone's blahs and ho-hums? If you find yourself getting sucked into someone else's toilet bowl of despair, it's because you feel a sense of responsibility to fix them and make it better...or guilt that you caused it. It's not about you (no matter what they may tell you)! For today, practice empathy and compassion but leave the fix-its and guilt-ies at home.

When we are in a relationship, we each bring our "stuff" into it, and though we may not be aware of it, our "stuff" is driving our bus...choosing our behavior and causing our reactions. Other people might trigger our "stuff" but what we choose to do with it is 100% our own. It's not about your partner, or your kid, or your boss...it's about YOU. For today, when you find yourself reacting, breathe...and ask yourself who is driving.

"The walls we build around us to keep the sadness out also keep out the joy." ~Jim Rohn.
It's inevitable...we shield up to protect ourselves from getting hurt, but that same shield also protects us from the true connection of real intimacy. For today, let someone see you. Share a fear or a dream with someone you love. See if you can lower the walls a bit...or at least take the alligators out of the moat.

You are not alone...well, at least you don't have to be alone. Yes, our stories may be completely different, but our feelings are essentially the same. I feel sad, and silly, and scared, and hurt, and not good enough...just like you do. For today, give yourself the gift of connecting with another person...we're everywhere...all you have to do is reach out.

*"Make somebody happy today.
Mind your own business."
~Ann Landers.
What fun we have when we distract ourselves from ourselves by looking up everyone else's pants leg! It's so much easier to look at other people's problems, faults and lives than it is to focus on our own. For today, when you find yourself getting wrapped up in someone else's stuff, ask yourself what's happening on your side of the street.*

Relationships

We're afraid of being hurt, so we imprison ourselves behind walls in an attempt to control our lives and emotions. But control is an illusion we create to try and keep ourselves from feeling pain. The truth is that we will get hurt, people will disappoint us. Pain is as much a part of the human experience as joy. One of our goals here is to learn to trust ourselves enough to know that we will be ok, no matter what...that even when life hurts, tomorrow is another day. Ultimately, it's all about you taking care of you. Now THAT is freedom.

There's nothing like a road trip to remind me that attitude really IS everything. After a long (very, very long) trip, I was physically, mentally and emotionally exhausted and I could feel myself getting snarky and pouty and wanting to lash out at my partner...but then I remembered that the only one responsible for my well-being is ME. It's amazing how much kinder I could be when I remembered that it wasn't his fault that my back hurt. You've got YOU. ♥

*Warning: radical concept ahead! Other people's opinions of and reactions to you are none of your business. It's not your responsibility to manage the emotions of the people around you...that's their job. Your job is to be true to yourself, set and hold boundaries that work for you and live your life with love, kindness and compassion.
It's all about YOU!*

Relationships

"You have your way. I have my way. As for the right way, the correct way, and the only way, it does not exist."
~Friedrich Nietzsche.

When you find yourself consumed with another person's lifestyle or choices or behaviors, ask yourself why it's so important to you. We are all stumbling through life with more questions than answers...the least we can do is love each other along the way.

Comparing ourselves with others is so painful! A good rule of thumb is to remember that we all present our best selves to the world...our strengths rather than our weaknesses. I mean, seriously, no one puts pictures on Facebook of their kids running around screaming bloody murder, house a disaster area, wearing their torn t-shirts with spit up in their hair! When we compare what we feel to be our worst selves to what appears to be the best selves of others, we never win. For today, instead of comparing, try to find common ground. We are all beautifully imperfect! ♥

Oh, how we strive for perfection! We feel like something is wrong with us if we are not perfectly beautiful, strong, happy, rich and brilliant. No wonder we all feel so inadequate! What makes us beautiful IS our "imperfection"... our human struggles, emotions, insecurities. What would our world look like if we stopped pretending we had it all together and allowed ourselves to be vulnerable with one another?

Life is so much easier when we are able to speak the truth for ourselves...think about how much energy and time you have lost by getting "stuck" in situations or conversations you didn't want to be involved in. And how quickly did your resignation turn to anger and resentment at the person who "trapped" you? Just say NO! You never, ever have to be a victim of anyone or anything. Breathe, smile and walk away. ♥

Watching those we love struggle is so hard. We want to "fix" it, to "make it better"...partly because seeing them in pain is so painful for us, but the most supportive thing we can do is just let them be where they are and love them. We all have a right to our feelings...and the right to express those feelings however we need to. How many times have you stifled your emotions so that someone else wouldn't feel badly?

*Every day is a new opportunity...
a chance to connect with people
through love...to see and be seen.
Whether it's an old friend you
haven't seen for a while or a new
one who is just beginning in your
life, take the opportunity to connect
from the heart. See them...let them
see you. And for today...go
forth and LOVE!* ♥

Trust, Intimacy, Vulnerability... oh, my! Some days I would much rather deal with lions, tigers and bears. It seems safer for us to connect with each other intellectually. No risk of rejection, no fear of a broken heart. But also, no real connection. So for today, even though I'm scared, I'm ready to have people in my life who see me and let me see them. It's a whole new world. We're not in Kansas anymore, Toto!

Forget the 3 R's...today let's focus on the 3 A's: Acknowledge, Accept and Allow. When faced with "difficult" emotions, we usually want them to go away as quickly as possible...but the problem with ignoring them is that they tend to come back bigger and stronger. If we can simply acknowledge them, accept that we are human and allow ourselves to just be where we are, things tend to be a little less overwhelming.

After we practice using the 3 A's (Acknowledge, Accept and Allow) on ourselves, we can begin to apply the same concepts to others in our lives. Sometimes it's harder to accept that their path is THEIR path...it's not about us, whether we agree with them or not. So, we can acknowledge them, accept that they are human and allow them to just be where they are with no judgment and lots of love.

Relationships

We're taught young that love is performance based...get good grades, smile pretty...behave. And we carry that belief with us as adults...work harder, do more, smile pretty...behave. Afraid that no one will love us if we drop the smile and show real emotion, we fake it, forgetting that all of us have those same emotions. Wouldn't it be nice to drop the act and connect with each other as living, breathing, feeling humans?

How many times have I heard my partner's tone and assumed he was annoyed with me when it had nothing to do with me at all? We assume people don't like us, that they think we're fat, that we are incompetent. We project our insecurities and "stuff" onto others and then we shut down and pull away. For today, give yourself the benefit of the doubt...assume you are beautiful and fabulous and that everyone else thinks so, too!

Relationships

We spend so much energy trying to "manage" ourselves so that other people won't be upset or angry or put out by our "issues." We go over conversations incessantly, we stifle our needs, we do things we do not want to do...all in the name of peace. And then we are angry at THEM for making us feel bad. Please, please... for today, ask yourself, "what about ME?" And then listen. ♥

Relationships

Take a look at the people in your life today and see if you can feel the overwhelming love they have for you. If the world is our mirror then what we see looking back at us is strength, beauty, support, tenderness, acceptance...real people with real emotions who are doing the best they can each day to live their lives in love.
WOW...we look GOOD!

Relationships

We are all pretty clear about our physical boundaries-if someone gets too close physically, we feel uncomfortable and back up. But, what about energetic and emotional boundaries? How many times have you done something you really didn't want to do "for" someone else? Were you then angry at the person you were doing it "for"? It's ok to say NO. Just for today, see what it feels like to choose you.

We all have different stories, but our basic feelings are the same. We all have fear, grief, we are all unsure of ourselves, we all get lonely. And we are each essentially striving for the same thing...love, happiness, health, peace, prosperity. Just for today, see if you can look upon everyone you meet with compassion and love...with empathy...knowing that they too, are doing the best they can with what they have. You don't have to do this alone.

Look at your interactions with others. Do you find yourself stuck in the fun game of "Who's the Bigger Victim"? Going back and forth about who has it worse? Venting with someone else about your job/husband/mother/health may feel better in the moment, but it's really just a way to keep yourself angry and resentful. For today, see it you can let go of the Victim Game and use that energy to make positive changes for YOU.

I am responsible for me. When I try to adjust my feelings/actions/decisions to "keep other people happy", I end up resentful, frustrated and angry and then no one is happy. For today, I remember that my job is to keep ME happy and everything else will fall into place.

Relationships

The other day I was standing perfectly still when someone smacked right into me...ouch! So, what did I say? "I'm sorry!"...what?? Why? Why do we do that? We don't want people to feel badly, but every time we apologize for simply standing still we tell ourselves that the other person's feelings are more important than ours. For today, pay attention to what you are apologizing for...

How much energy do we spend trying to manage other people's emotions? A lot! We "assume" that someone doesn't want to help us or that their feelings will be hurt or they'll be mad. And they might be any or all of those things...but if they are, it's none of your business! Your job is to manage YOU and their job is to manage THEM. Ta-da! Energy crisis solved.

Relationships

Sometimes life just wears us down...we feel physically heavier, so tired. We wonder how we got here, what we're doing and when it's going to get better. When we get to this place (I call it the toilet bowl of despair), many times we want to isolate, to run away to an island. But remember, we need each other. For today, let someone see you... really see you. Maybe life will feel a little lighter. ♥

I'm working on the I-word... Intimacy. Allowing the people in my life to really see me...and not just the "good" me, but also my fears, my sadness. This is proving to be a really scary process and I'm finding that it's all about trust...not about trusting THEM, but trusting myself enough to know that I'll be ok no matter what happens with other people.

We would all like for our partners and friends to look lovingly at us and say, "gee, you look overloaded...how can I help you?"...and sometimes they do. But we cannot wait for other people to notice that we need help. You have words...use them. For today, instead of getting angry because no one is reading your mind or listening to your deep sighs of annoyance, speak up! Ask for what you need... you just might get it!

Responsibility...I always hear that word in a deep, booming voice inside my head. I used to be confused about its meaning...I thought it meant sacrificing myself and taking care of everyone else. The truth is, I am responsible for ME... for my actions, feelings, needs and wants. It has nothing to do with taking care of everyone ELSE's feelings or needs. For today, be responsible...take care of YOU.

Why are we so concerned with what other people think? It's really none of our business. Would you act differently if other people weren't judging you? Would you speak up more? Laugh louder? Quit that job you hate to write a novel? For today, see if you can worry less about what everyone else thinks and focus on the only opinion that really matters. Yours. ♥

It's better to be honest than weird. Someone hurts your feelings...you get angry. Suddenly you find yourself feeling pouty and acting snarky. Days go by...everything they do makes you more annoyed...you want to strangle them and you can't remember why. What if instead of being weird you could have been honest in the moment and spoken up about your hurt feelings? Less energy wasted, for sure!

We are such funny creatures...we bounce back and forth between feeling like we're less than everyone else to feeling like everyone else is an idiot because they're not doing things "our" way. That's one of the beautiful things about being human...we are not just one dimensional...our "crazyville" can multitask! (wink) The key here is to bring our focus back to ourselves with the gentle reminder that we're perfect just the way we are...and so is "everyone else".

Being responsible is not the same as TAKING responsibility for others. We spend our days anticipating what other people may want, assuming how they may feel, attempting to mold ourselves into what we think they need us to be...whew! No wonder we are so exhausted. Try this on for size today: just be YOU. Focus on what YOU want...what YOU feel...and what YOU need you to be. And let everyone else do the same for them. Whoa...weird!

Compassion

Compassion

I don't believe in mistakes...I try to remember that even those "what was I thinking?!?" moments occur for a reason. Looking back, I know that had I not made some of those "mistakes", I wouldn't be where I am right now...and I wouldn't trade my right now for anything. For today, take a look back and see where your "mistakes" have brought you...not so bad, huh?

Compassion

Be gentle with yourself. And with others. This path we walk is difficult...sometimes painful, sometimes lonely. Every day we do the best we can with what we have...and so does everyone else. For today, set yourself up for success...lower your "perfect" standard and give yourself a break. You are right where you are supposed to be doing exactly what you are supposed to be doing... learning and living. Breathe...

Compassion

I'm a strong, independent woman. Sometimes, however, that independence turns to stubbornness and does more harm than good. It is so difficult for me to ask for help. I'm afraid to show vulnerability or be less than superwoman. But when I step into that place, I end up pushing everyone away and feel worse. So for today, I'm lowering my walls and utilizing my amazing support system. Send in the positive energy, please!

Compassion

Wise words shared by a wise woman..."you used to be tough, but now you are strong." Tough means putting up walls, porcupine spikes, and our armadillo shells...strength comes from taking down our protective shields and facing the world with softness and vulnerability, knowing that we may get hurt but safe and secure in the fact that we can handle ourselves no matter what. Vulnerable ≠ Victim. Our strength comes from love. ♥

Compassion

"Someday perhaps the inner light will shine forth from within us, and then we'll need no other light."
~Goethe.

Do you have any idea how amazing you are? You are kind and beautiful and talented and smart in ways that no other person will ever be. When is the last time you gave yourself credit for all the fabulous things you do? For today...flip your switch, turn on your light and let everyone see you shine. ♥

Compassion

Right this minute, you are exactly WHO you are supposed to be, doing exactly WHAT you are supposed to be doing. Your choices are yours alone and they lead you to the exact path you need to be on for that moment in time. Life is hard enough without our constant judgment of ourselves. For today, remember that every choice you make is just perfect for right now. You're doing everything right. Good job!

Compassion

We forget sometimes that we have everything we need...right inside of us. You are wise beyond your years, have strength beyond your wildest dreams, and the magical power to shape and heal your life no matter what your circumstances. Yes, you. It's called love. For today, breathe from your heart, not your head.

We strive for happiness...we struggle for serenity-and we're frustrated because after all this work, we end up right back where we started. Clients tell me, "but I've been working so hard to find balance!" ...and that, sometimes, is the problem. Our brow is furrowed, our shoulders hunched...ouch! Relax...let go...breathe...it doesn't have to be so hard. For today, take a break and let the happiness find YOU.

Compassion

Every moment that you choose to take care of yourself...every time you make a conscious effort to slow down and breathe, you are making your world a better place. Change doesn't always come with huge fanfare...sometimes it's the collection of little things that add up to create the biggest shifts. For today, give yourself credit for those "little" things...

Compassion

Be gentle, be kind, be loving...to yourself! What does that mean? Start with the basics...allow yourself to rest when you are tired, eat balanced, healthy foods, breathe...do what you can to quiet that harsh, judgmental voice in your head that insists you are not enough. Remind yourself that you have a right to your feelings...all of them. You are beautiful, amazing and miraculous...just the way you are. ♥

Compassion

So, I'm ready to change...how do I do that? Where do I start? Remember that learning a new behavior is a skill...just like playing the piano or learning a new language. We don't decide we want to speak Swahili one day and wake up fluent in it the next. It's a process that takes practice, patience and dedication. And we are not perfect...ever. So for today, cut yourself some slack and don't give up!

Compassion

No matter what part of the world we live in...Europe, Asia, South America, the Middle East or the US...we all look upon the same Moon. And for all of us, She represents peace, serenity, power, intuition and unity. For today, wherever you are, take a moment to look up at her full face and remember that we are all connected and you are never alone.
Om Chandraya Namaha.

Compassion

"We are our greatest enemy. If we had our way, we would cut ourselves to pieces in order to remove what was unacceptable." ~Osho.

As we come to awareness of our "heavy" emotions, our first question is "how do I get rid of them?". True living, true enlightenment...is getting to know ALL of ourselves and then learning to love each part. No matter what. ♥

Compassion

Today, I remember to have FUN! When I'm leading with my heart, everything is easy, joyful, filled with light and love...I'm sure of myself and my path. But, when I get up into my head insecurities, doubt and fear take over and that wrinkle in my forehead gets more pronounced. So, for today I'm stepping back into my heart...today I choose to hand over the doubt and just enjoy the ride!

Compassion

It's wonderful that we want to become better people, to learn, to stretch, to grow...but in all this self-improvement, remember that you are pretty fabulous just the way you are. Yes, there is always room for improvement but even if you never changed a thing you are pretty amazing. The funny thing is that when we are able to accept ourselves as we are, the change we so desperately want becomes a little easier. ♥

Compassion

"Try not. Do, or do not...there is no try." ~Yoda.
The little green man is very wise... our "trying" leads to frustration. When you are ready, you'll do it (whatever it is for you) and not a moment sooner. The judgment we place on ourselves for "failing" is what is painful. For today, give yourself a break and know that you are right where you are supposed to be.

Compassion

I used to think there was a "grown up" manual that everyone had access to but me...that I was the only one feeling lost and clueless. Now I know that there is no manual...we all just do the best we can. Not having all the answers is scary, but normal. Just for today ...give yourself a break...the path you walk may not always be perfect, but it is your path and it's all going to be ok.

Compassion

Today I remember that I am human and that perfection is not what I'm striving for. I don't have all the answers and honestly, I'm not sure I want them. I want the human experience and all that comes with it: joy, pain, love, sadness, fear, peace, anger...all of it. We can't have light without dark and what I know for sure is that even in the dark, this too shall pass and we are all going to be okay.

Compassion

Do you know that you are amazing? Beautiful? A perfect child of the Universe? You are love, light, joy. You are abundance, power, divinity. Not because of WHAT you are, but because you ARE. Yes, you! I'm talking to you. You deserve to love and be loved. No matter what.

Compassion

Why is it that we can take such good care of ourselves for a few days or weeks and then slide right back into old behavior? We tell ourselves stories: it's easier to go through the drive-thru; I don't have the money; I don't have time; someone else should do this for me. Taking care of ourselves is HARD ...it requires commitment and effort every day...and we have to believe that we deserve it. Tell yourself you are WORTH it!

Compassion

What if you were to never, ever change anything about yourself again? What if you were to stay exactly where you are right now? Same weight, same outlook, same job, same relationships? And what if you are okay just the way you are? It's wonderful that we want to grow and change and improve but don't forget to love and accept yourself just as you are today. You are enough. And you are beautiful.

Compassion

We are bombarded with "helpful" tips...how to find inner peace, what to eat, how to exercise, how to talk to one another, do this, do that...EEEK!! We go after "self-improvement" like piranhas after a meal. Motivation is a wonderful thing, but it's easy to go overboard and burn ourselves out. For today...remember that our goal here is balance and that sometimes, less is more. Breathe...

Compassion

Love is in the air and "you as much as anyone in the universe, deserve your love and attention." ~Buddha. We love to love others, but struggle with loving ourselves. Just for today take a little bit (or a lot!) of the love you give out to everyone in your life and point it at you. If you can let your love IN, you'll find you have so much more to give OUT. You have the right to love and be loved, and it starts with you!

Compassion

Your homework for today is to stop right now and decide what nice, loving, comforting thing you are going to do for yourself this weekend. Give yourself permission to celebrate yourself...a hot bath with lavender, an hour or two with a good book, lunch with dear friend. It doesn't have to be complicated or expensive...just do something you love. You deserve it! ♥

Compassion

Human beings need touch. The touch of another person can calm us, lower our blood pressure, release tension. But interestingly, our culture (especially American culture) frowns upon asking for comfort. It makes us look weak, or (god forbid!) needy. When is the last time you asked for a hug? Or allowed yourself to just lay your head on someone's shoulder? For today, reach out and touch someone...doctor's orders! ♥

Compassion

I'm always surprised at how triggering it is for me to be physically ill. I feel "bad" for feeling bad...like I've done something wrong. I feel guilty for being human even though I spend every day reminding all of us that our beauty is IN our humanness. For today, my gentle reminder is to show myself the same compassion and love I show to the rest of the world.

Compassion

Stop. Just. Stop. For a few seconds...stop worrying...stop thinking...stop moving...just stop. Now breathe...seriously. Do it. Breathe...in through your nose...as slowly and as deeply as you can. Now hold it...just for a second. And let it go...let it all go. The weight of the world on your shoulders...let it go. The unspoken words in your clenched jaw...let them go. 20 seconds just for YOU...completely free totally portable and very effective. Repeat as needed for peace.

Compassion

Our stories and our circumstances may be different, but we are the same. We all fear that we are not enough, we all want to love and be loved...we feel joy, love, grief, stress. No matter religious or spiritual beliefs (or lack thereof), skin color, hometown. No matter sexual preferences, education, political beliefs. For today, remember that although our paths may be different, we are all on the same team.
Namaste.

www.ingramcontent.com/pod-product-compliance
Lightning Source LLC
Chambersburg PA
CBHW061303110426
42742CB00012BA/2041